MUSICIANS INSTITUTE™

MASTER CLASS

Modern Jazz Concepts
for Guitar

Innovative Improvisation Techniques

By Sid Jacobs

Edited by Arthur Rotfeld

ISBN 0-634-04825-2

HAL•LEONARD®
CORPORATION

7777 W. BLUEMOUND RD. P.O. BOX 13819 MILWAUKEE, WI 53213

In Australia Contact:
Hal Leonard Australia Pty. Ltd.
22 Taunton Drive P.O. Box 5130
Cheltenham East, 3192 Victoria, Australia
Email: ausadmin@halleonard.com

Visit Hal Leonard Online at
www.halleonard.com

Contents

Introduction

"The Tao that can be told is not the eternal Tao."— Lao-tzu

Jazz improvisation is a language and as such, vocabulary doesn't necessarily accomplish communication. As students on a musical path, we are challenged to broaden our expressive palette. In the beginning we learn basic tools and principles. As we grow our artistic senses become more refined. Learning new techniques and means of expression can stimulate creativity. Eventually we can choose to use or abandon a learned technique because we are operating more directly from the source. The goal—and that word is inadequate, as it implies the path has an end—is freedom of expression. Freedom comes from discipline. That's the paradox. Part of the art is to learn the craft. The natural balance is upset when the technique is noticed before the music.

Advanced Guitar Improvisation deals with some sophisticated and important concepts and vocabulary used by jazz musicians today. The discussions of each topic are intended as a brief conceptual overview. These ideas are presented to be a catalyst in your creative process.

Voice Leading Melodic Lines

When I began playing jazz, a great player (not a guitarist) told me that he thought of chord voicings when he played lines. At the time this information did not connect with my way of thinking. I was playing root position chords, unaware of any voice leading. When I became aware of guide tones—the 7th of a chord resolving to the 3rd of the following chord—and applied the concept, my playing was transformed.

These preliminary examples present chord voicings and related single note lines. Play each progression, getting comfortable with the sound and fingering before playing the lines.

Here is the common ii–V–I–vi progression, using rootless voicings, and presented with careful voice leading.

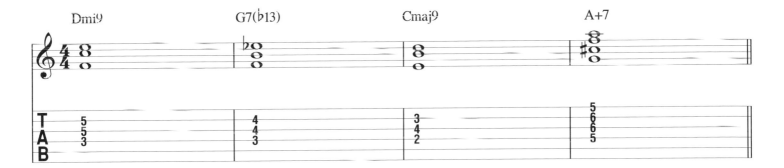

This is a linear presentation of the same harmony and voice leading. Notice how the voicings are broken into lines and ornamented with occasional passing and neighbor tones.

This example uses some ii–V cycles and a steady eighth-note line.

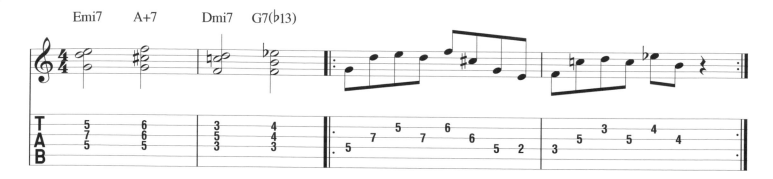

This example also uses ii–V cycles. This time a triplet-based line is developed.

The voicings in this example move around more, hence the related line is more active.

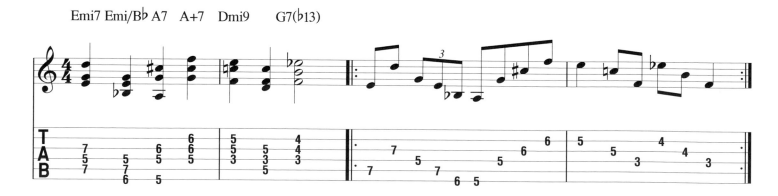

This example uses a common minor key progression, where the tonic chord is heard over a chromatically descending bass. The rhythmically angular line clearly presents the sweeping contour of each voicing.

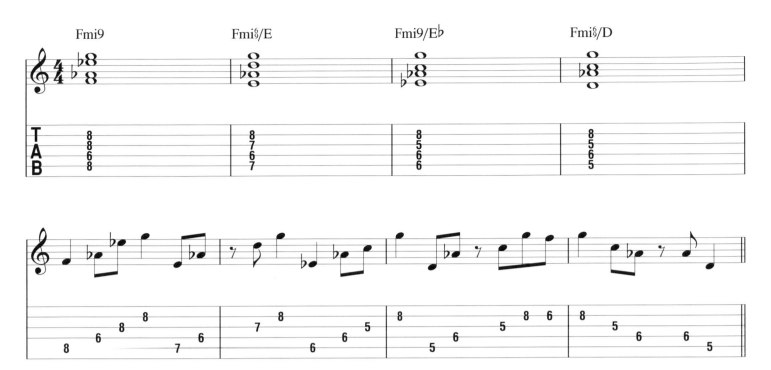

Here's the same figure in 3/4 time. Notice that the rhythmic idea from the previous example is used again, but here it lines up more predictably with the meter.

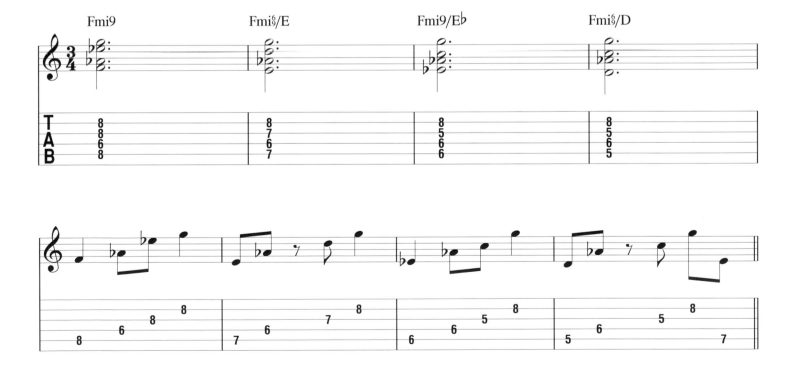

The basic "rhythm changes" I–vi–ii–V progression, with some chord alterations, is presented here. A wide-spanning, triplet-filled line follows.

This progression (I–V/IV–IV–♭VII–I) is also from the rhythm changes A-section.

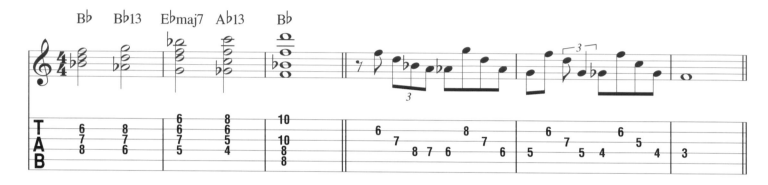

Here is something based on the rhythm changes bridge progression—just a sequence of dominant chords moving around the circle of fifths.

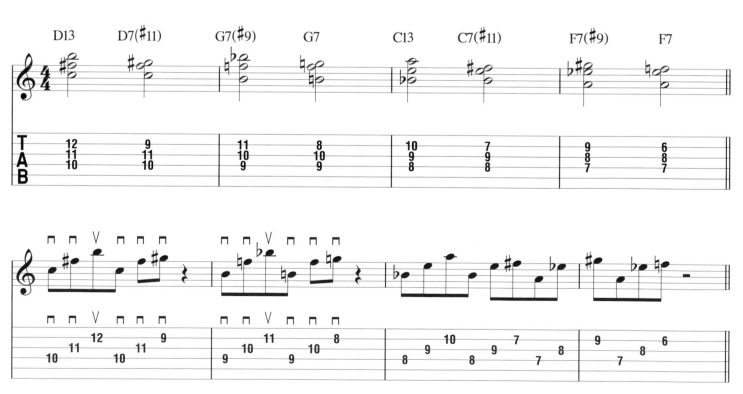

Symmetrical Scales

In addition to the various diatonic scales (including the major and minor scales as well as their modes), jazz musicians have been using a variety of symmetrical scales for decades. The symmetry comes from dividing the octave into equal parts to form each specific scale. By its inherent nature, a symmetrical scale can always be known by other roots. (For example, a C whole tone scale contains the exact same notes as a D, E, F♯, G♯, or A♯ whole tone scale, and accordingly, it can be named by any of those notes.)

The octave (a distance of 12 semitones, or half steps) can be divided in half at the tritone (as its name suggests, three tones, or six semitones).

Dividing the octave into three parts, or major thirds, (a distance of four semitones) yields an augmented triad.

Dividing the octave into four parts, or minor thirds (a distance of three semitones), yields a diminished seventh chord.

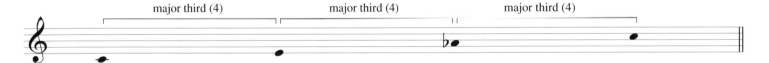

Dividing the octave into six parts, or major seconds (a distance of two semitones), yields a whole tone scale. This is the simplest symmetrical scale, one consisting entirely of whole steps.

Other symmetrical scales can be easily constructed by adding half steps below each of the dividing notes.

The tetratonic (four note) scale is based on the tritone interval. To construct the scale a half step is added below each note of the tritone. The symmetry forms a pattern of perfect 4th–half step. There are six different tetratonic scales. This example is the C tetratonic scale, but it also can be viewed as the G♭ tetratonic scale.

The augmented scale is constructed from the major third interval. A half step is added below each note of the augmented triad to form the scale. The symmetry is based on the pattern minor 3rd–half step. There are four different augmented scales. This example is the C augmented scale, but it can also be viewed as the E or A♭ augmented scale.

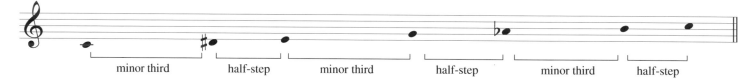

Here is the diminished scale. To construct this scale a half step is added below each note of the diminished seventh chord. The symmetry forms a pattern of whole step-half step. There are three different diminished scales. This example is the C diminished scale, but it also can be viewed as the E♭, G♭, or A diminished scale.

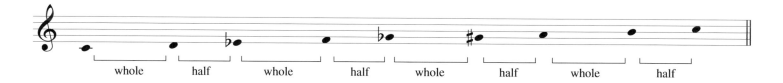

The whole tone scale is a symmetrical scale, as all notes are a whole step apart. Preceding each note of this scale with another note would yield the chromatic scale. Any note in this scale could be viewed as the root. There are only two different whole tone scales.

The Tetratonic Scale

Just as any five-note scale qualifies as pentatonic, any four-note scale is tetratonic. Here however, we will limit ourselves to the tetratonic symmetrical scale based on the tritone. This tetratonic scale (along with the other non-diatonic scales we'll study) is useful to the jazz musician in how it can be used to alter traditional harmonic situations.

There are six different tritone intervals (not counting the inversions), and from each a different tetratonic symmetrical scale can be built. Here are the six different scales:

First let's look at some logical fingerings of the scale. Three possible left-hand fingerings are given.

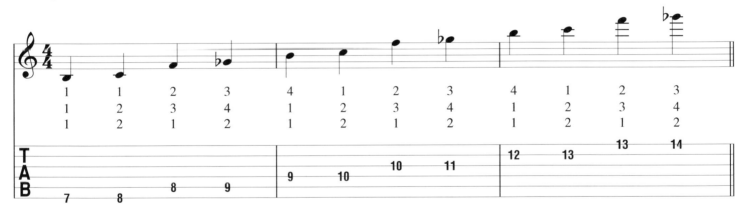

Here is a fingering that will allow some sweep picking and smooth phrasing.

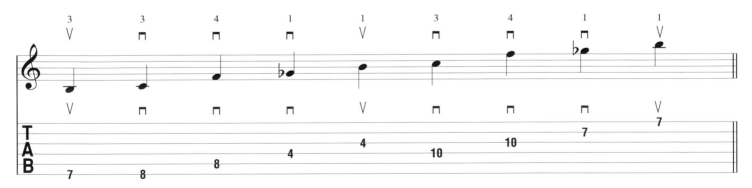

Track 1 This is a simple linear presentation of the tetratonic scale, using sweep picking when possible.

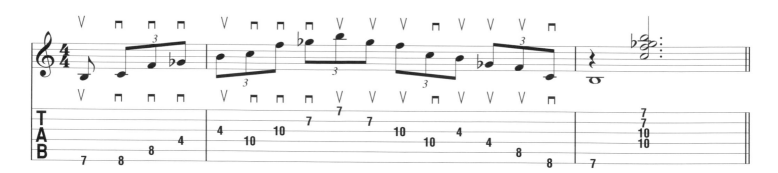

 Track 2 This line is comprised of the two tritone pairs found in the tetratonic scale.

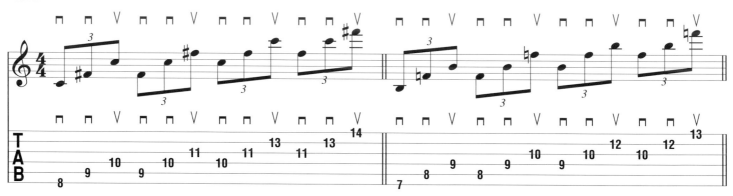

 Track 3 Here is a more fleshed-out version of the previous example. Here the two-tritone-pairs idea is developed with the use of inversions.

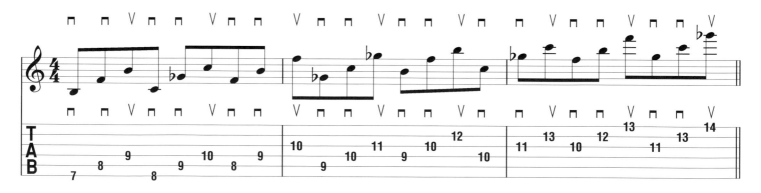

Track 4

This is a more complex pattern, ascending in one tritone pair and descending in another.

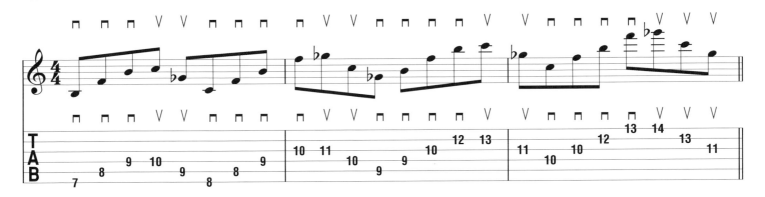

Track 5

Here a melodic idea is presented and then sequenced downward by a tritone. Of course all notes are still within the scale.

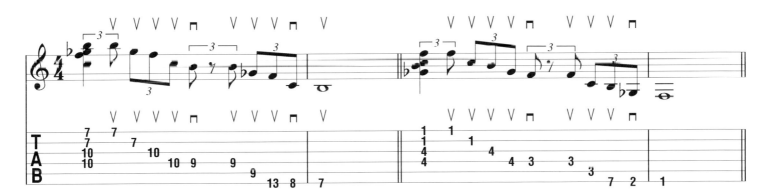

Track 6

This example presents a four-note motive that is sequenced upward by tritones.

Track 7 Here a slightly more complex motive is sequenced upward by tritones.

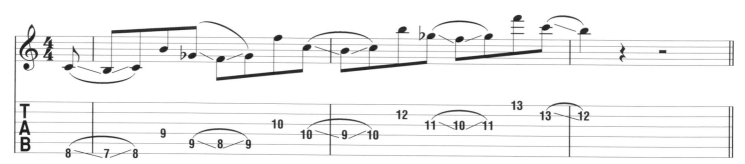

Track 8 Here a simple, descending motive is sequenced downward by tritones.

Track 9 Here are some four-note chords from the tetratonic scale. The chords are followed by a sequence of dyads (two-note groups) that is based on the four-note chord shapes.

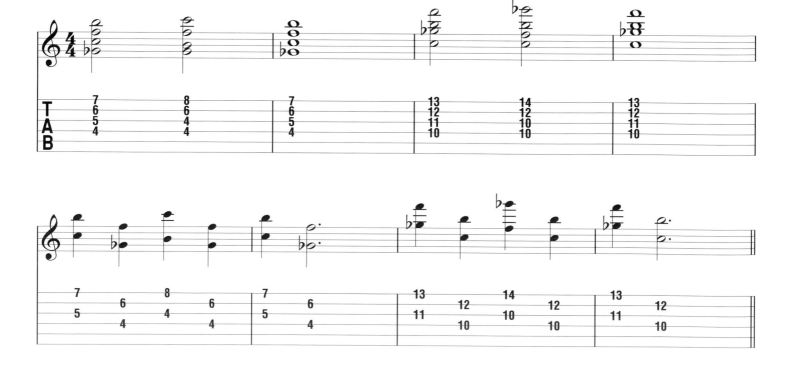

Let's look at a practical application of the tetratonic scale. The C tetratonic scale contains the notes C, F, G♭, and B. The C and G♭ (F♯) are the color tones, the 7th and 3rd, of a D7 chord. The other two notes, B and F, are the 13th and ♯9th.

By using tritone substitution (in which a dominant chord is substituted for another dominant chord a tritone away), we arrive at the same result.

	C	F	G♭	B
A♭7	3	13	♭7	♯9
D7	♭7	♯9	3	13

You might have noticed that the tetratonic scale contains half the notes of the diminished scale. Notice how it can be used over two more dominant chords—the two other dominants from the diminished scale. It's not quite as colorful, as it yields roots and 5ths, but it does offer ♭9ths and ♯11ths.

	C	F	G♭	B
B7	♭9	♯11	5	R
F7	5	R	♭9	♯11

Play all of the tetratonic lines and apply them to each of the four dominant chords. In this case, A♭7, D7, B7, and F7.

Now let's develop more complex chords and lines.

Each note of the tetratonic scale can be harmonized with a tritone, so here is a scalar figure comprised of tritone dyads.

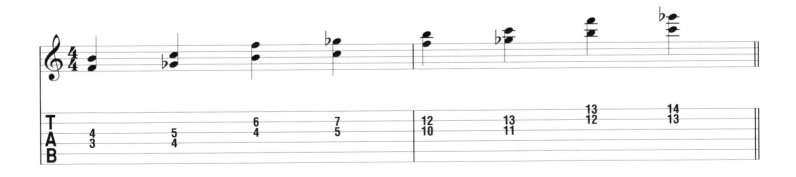

Track 10 We can break up larger chord shapes into smaller ones. Here each four-note voicing is divided into two three-note shapes.

Here a three-note chord is given. This voicing is then used as the basis for harmonizing the scale. Notice how each voice (low, middle, and high) traces a scalar line.

Track 11 This is a line based on the same voicings given above.

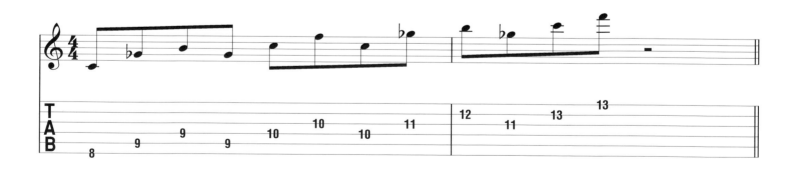

The Augmented Scale

The augmented scale consists of two augmented triads a minor third apart. The scale shown below contains C augmented and D# augmented. Because the scale is symmetrical at the major third, any sequence of notes or chords can be transposed up or down a major third and remain within the scale. So while it is easy to create melodic patterns using symmetrical scales, the challenge is avoiding the predictable—the death of art.

Here is the C augmented scale, based on C.

This example shows that each note of the augmented scale can be harmonized with an augmented triad.

The augmented scale can also yield three major and three minor triads.

Other chords, such as major 7ths and major 7#5 are found in the scale.

Here are some useful fingerings for the augmented scale.

The augmented scale offers an alternative, non-diatonic way of experiencing a major 7th chord. Four notes from the scale are in the chord, while two are "outside." Of course the same can be said of any major 7th chord from the scale—this is symmetry.

Here is a chart showing the notes of the augmented scale and how they relate to the three major 7th chords the scale contains.

	C	D♯	E	G	A♭	B
Cmaj7	Root	#9	3	5	#5	7
Emaj7	#5	7	Root	#9	3	5
A♭maj7	3	5	#5	7	Root	#9

Track 12

When all three major or minor triads are played, all of the notes in the scale are used. This line is based on three major triads in root position. Try playing this line over Cmaj7, Emaj7, and A♭maj7. Be aware of the obvious similarities and subtle differences as you play this line against each chord.

Track 13

This line is based on the three major triads in first inversion.

Track 14

This line is based on the three major triads in second inversion. Also notice the use of a scale tone between each arpeggio.

Track 15

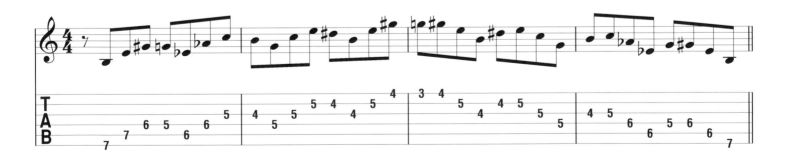

Track 16

This line is based on the three minor triads in root position.

Track 17

Here is a line based on the three maj7#5 chords.

Track 18

This line is also based on the three maj7#5 chords, this time in an ascending pattern.

This example uses ascending and descending augmented triads.

Track 19

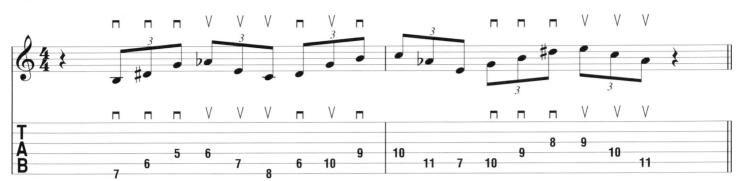

Augmented triads are used to make four-note phrases in this line.

Track 20

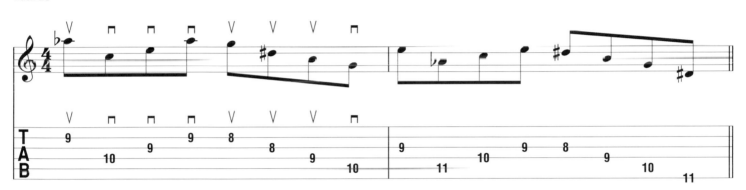

Maj7(#5) arpeggios reign supreme in this ascending line.

Track 21

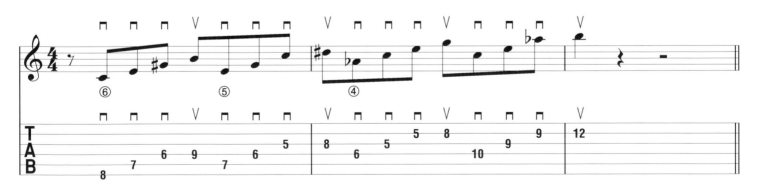

A simple figure of descending maj7(#5) arpeggios is presented in this line.

Track 22

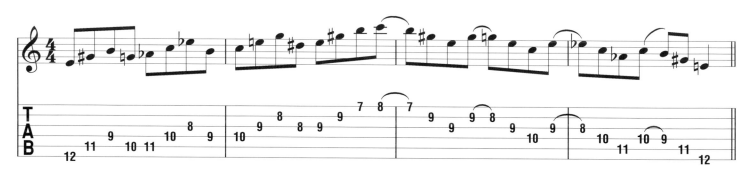

Notice the use of a scale tone between each maj7(#5) arpeggio in this line.

Track 23

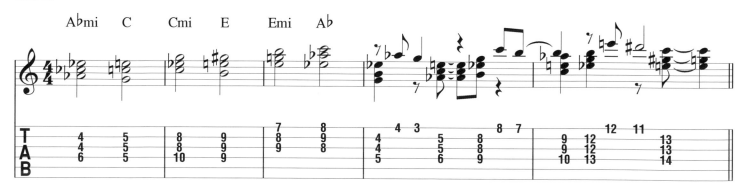

Chord shapes and patterns can be moved symmetrically as well.

Track 24

Some more unusual chord types, such as maj7(#9) and maj6(♭9) are also found in the augmented scale.

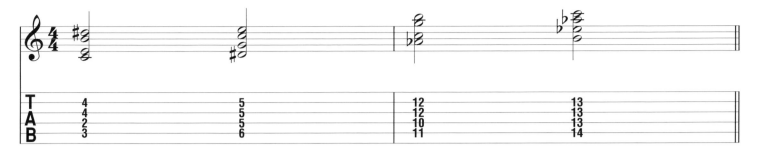

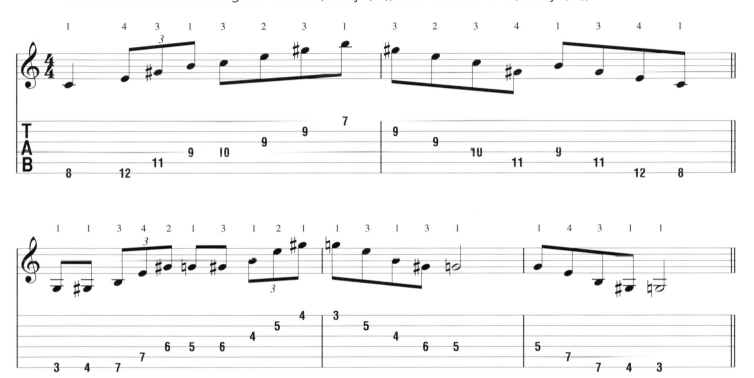

Chords over bass notes, so-called slash chords, are found in the augmented scale as well. Naturally these can be transposed by major thirds and still remain within the same harmonic environment. Here is a figure for E/C (Cmaj7(#5)) and one for E/G (Gmaj6(♭9)).

Track 25

Coltrane's "Giant Steps" is a progression based on three different major key resolutions in a major third relationship. The augmented scale can be used as a scale source and yield interesting results. This line, over the first three measures, uses G major and minor triads. These arpeggios establish extended chords over the dominant harmonies—B♭13(♭9) and

Track 26

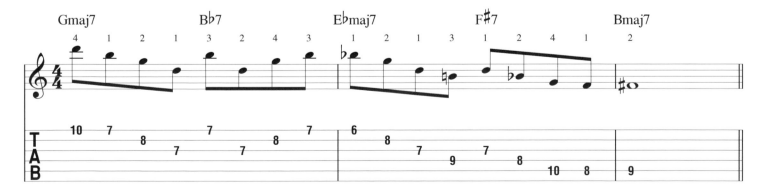

The Diminished Scale

The diminished scale consists of two diminished seventh chords a whole step apart. The scale shown below contains C diminished and D diminished. Because the scale is symmetrical at the minor third, any sequence of notes or chords can be transposed up or down a minor third and remain within the scale.

Here is the diminished scale, based on C.

Track 27 The descending part of this example includes half-step approaches to the symmetric minor thirds of the C diminished seventh arpeggio.

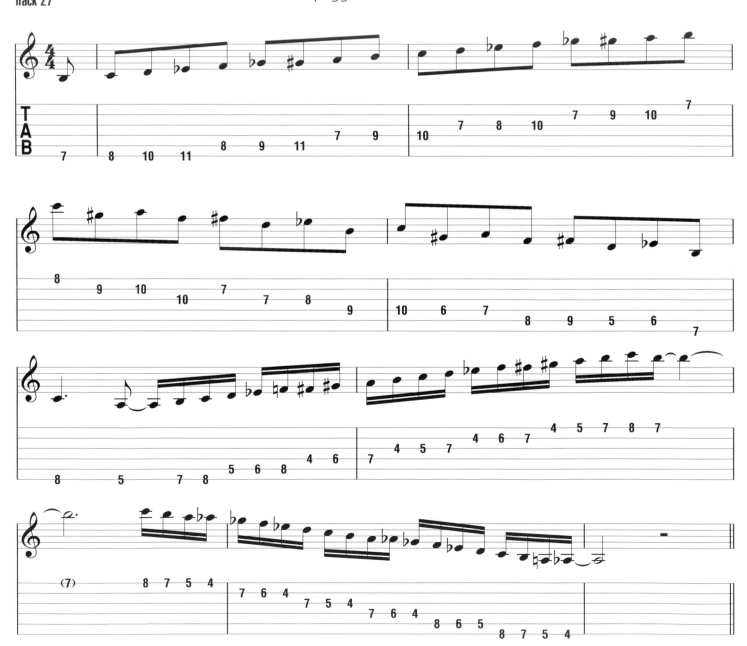

Each note of the diminished scale can be harmonized with a diminished seventh chord. The first two chords contain all eight notes of the scale.

Here a four-note voicing is given and is then used as the basis for harmonizing the scale. Notice how each voice (bass, tenor, alto, and soprano) follows a scalar line. An arpeggiated version of the same chords follows in the second staff.

Track 28

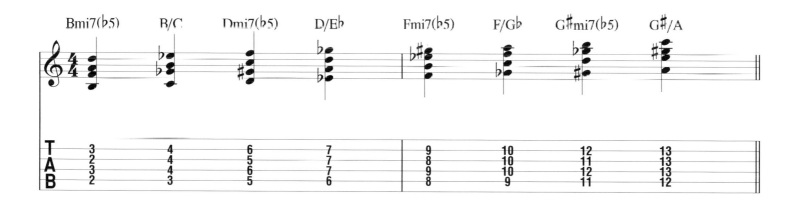

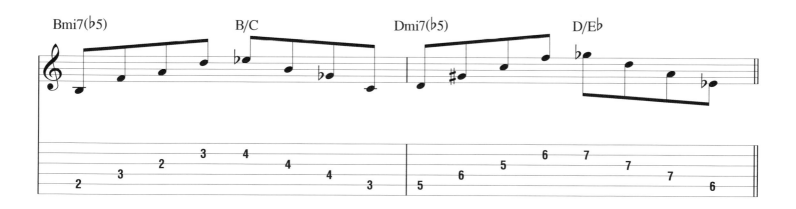

This diagram shows how the diminished chord relates to the four dominant chords. Notice that the dominant chords are a minor third apart from each other.

	C	E♭	G♭	A
B7	♭9	3	5	♭7
D7	♭7	♭9	3	5
F7	5	♭7	♭9	3
A♭7	3	5	♭7	♭9

It is important to note that the diminished scale, when following the whole step-half step pattern, relates to diminished chords, but when following a half step-whole step pattern, relates to dominant chords. This means that the C diminished (whole step-half step) contains the same notes as B diminished (half step-whole step).

Here is a chart that shows the function of each scale tone over the dominant chords.

	C	D	E♭	F	G♭	G♯	A	B
B7	♭9	♯9	3	♯11	5	13	♭7	R
D7	♭7	R	♭9	♯9	3	♯11	5	13
F7	5	13	♭7	R	♭9	♯9	3	♯11
A♭7	3	♯11	5	13	♭7	R	♭9	♯9

Here are some practical fingerings for the diminished scale.

This diminished scale fingering uses four notes per string.

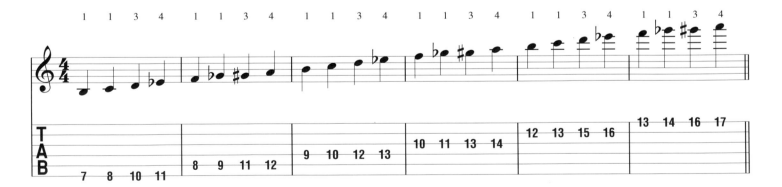

26

Here is a fingering that uses three notes per string.

Track 29

This diminished line is based on major triads a minor third apart.

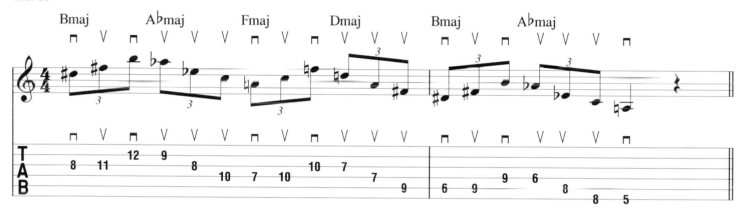

Track 30

This diminished line is based on minor triads a minor third apart.

Here is a cycle of two slash chords from the diminished scale. Notice how the shapes are duplicated as they ascend in minor thirds.

Track 31

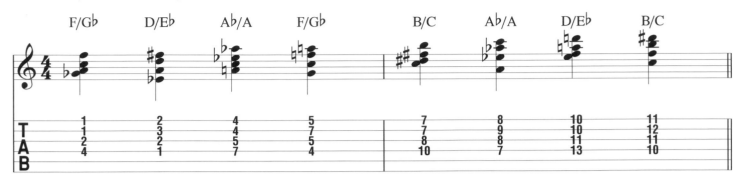

Sweep picking should be used for these diminished lines, which outline F/B and Ab/A. Try these lines over F7, D7, Ab7, or B7.

Track 32

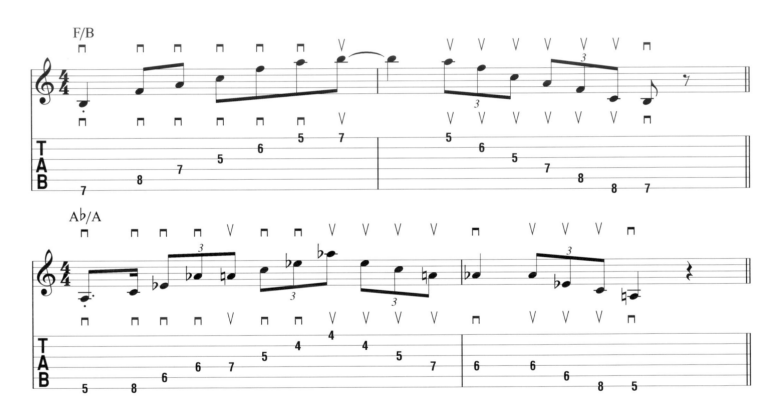

This triplet-based diminished line outlines D/Eb, F/Gb, and Ab/A. You can use this line over F7, D7, Ab7, or B7.

Track 33

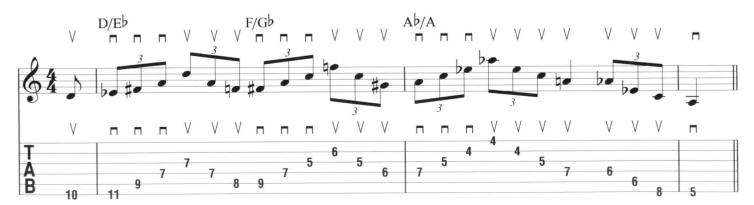

The Whole Tone Scale

The whole tone scale consists of two augmented triads a whole step apart. Each note in this six-note scale is a whole step away from the next, so any note of the scale can be considered the root. The whole tone scale is symmetrical by major seconds and any sequence of notes or chords from the scale can be moved up or down a major second and remain within the scale.

Here is the whole tone scale, based on C. Any of the other notes in the scale can also be considered the root.

Since there are only two scales, here is the other one, based on D♭. Again, any of the other notes in the scale can also be considered the root.

Every note in the whole tone scale can be harmonized by an augmented triad.

Here are two chord shapes from the whole tone scale in a pattern that ascends in whole steps. The melody created by the top notes alternates ascending and descending augmented fifths.

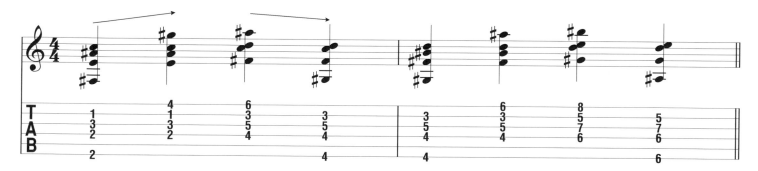

Here is a chart that shows the function of each scale tone over the dominant chords.

	C	D	E	F#	G#	A#
C7	R	9	3	#11	#5	♭7
D7	♭7	R	9	3	#11	#5
E7	#5	♭7	R	9	3	#11
F#7	#11	#5	♭7	R	9	3
G#7	3	#11	#5	♭7	R	9
B♭7	9	3	#11	#5	♭7	R

A three-note-per string fingering of the whole tone scale covers a lot of fingerboard.

Track 34

This line is based on two augmented triads a whole step apart.

Here is a more complex line, again based on two augmented triads a whole step apart.

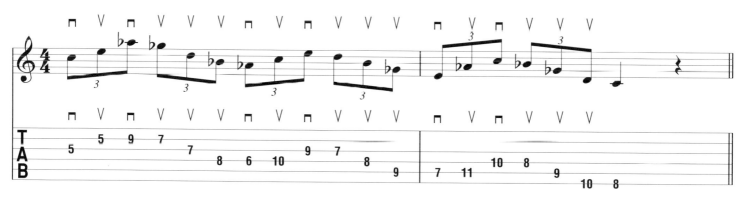

The symmetry inherent in the whole tone scale invites an ordered approach and predictable playing. It is wise to practice these ideas using rhythmic variety. Also, a simple pattern can become less predictable when a change of contour is applied to the sequence.

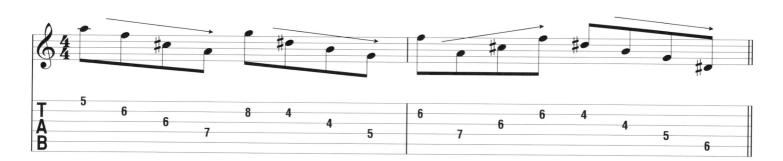

Here are a few melodic phrases that use the whole tone scale. All of these can be used over

Track 37 C7, D7, E7, F#7, A♭7, or B♭7.

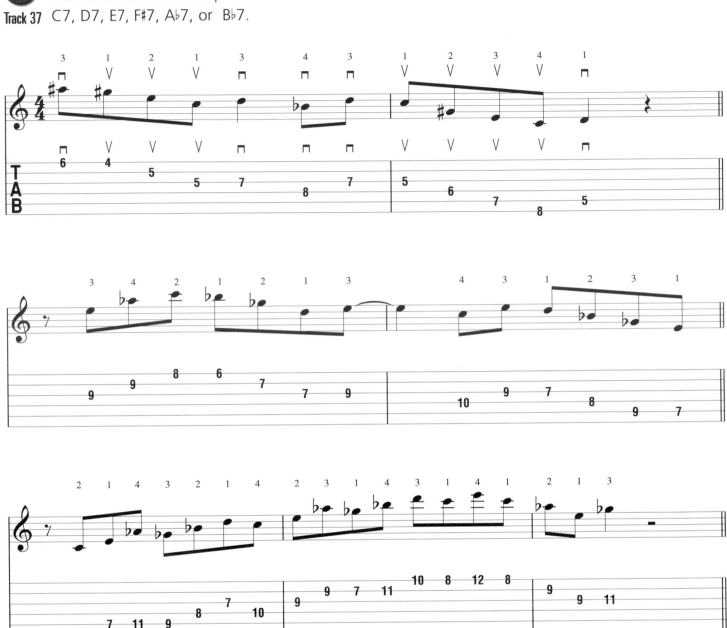

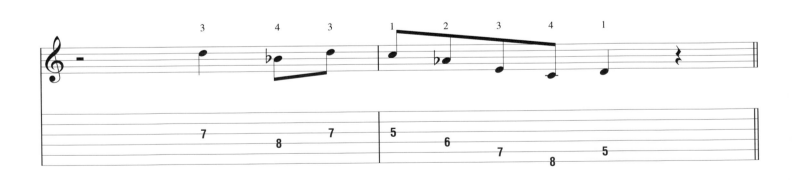

Track 38 Here is another whole tone line. After you learn one whole tone line, move it a half step away and you are in the other whole tone scale. Remember there are only two.

Track 39 Any melodic motive that contains an interval not in the scale (minor 2nds, minor 3rds, perfect 4ths, perfect 5ths, major 6ths, and major 7ths) that is sequenced using the whole tone scale results in a pattern using all twelve notes of the chromatic scale. Here a simple motive of a perfect fourth is sequenced down a C whole tone scale. To avoid the pitfalls of predictability, a change in contour is applied in the second line.

Triad Pairs

An important trend in modern jazz improvisation is the use of triad pairs. The concept is that the two triads, carefully chosen, yield six notes of a scale or mode. The intervallic approach gained by using triads helps contrast linear, scale-based playing.

The F and G Triad Pair

The F and G triad pair is from the C major scale and works well over C major or any of its modes. Since the E natural is not included, these triads may also be tried on C Dorian, C melodic minor, and related modalities.

Try the following F and G triad pair lines over Dmi7, G7, Fmaj7(#11), Cmi6/9, F13(#11), and B7 alt.

Track 40

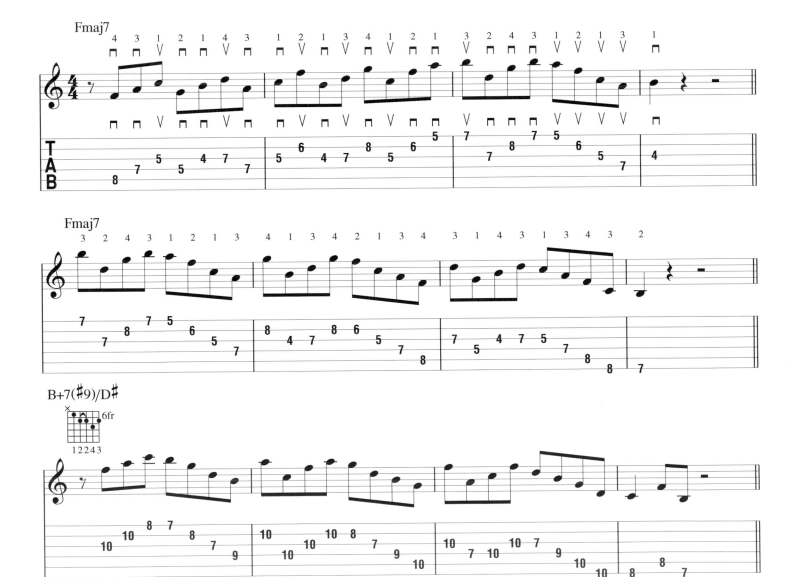

Here are F and G triads over a rising bass line, which gives us a variety of slash chords.

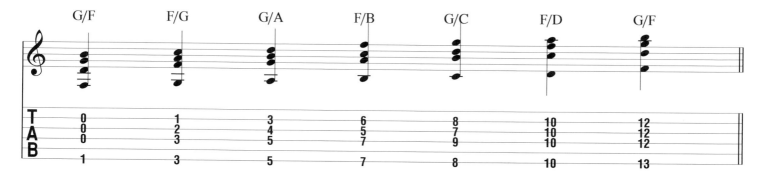

Here are the F and G triads over a rising bass line again, but a tighter harmony results from the triads being closer to the bass line.

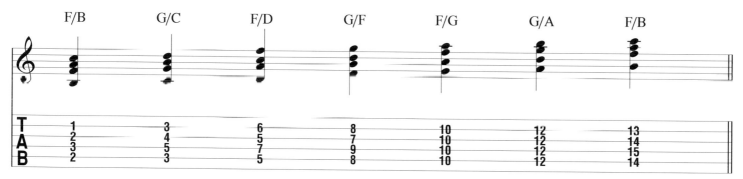

This time the "bass line" is placed on top of the triads.

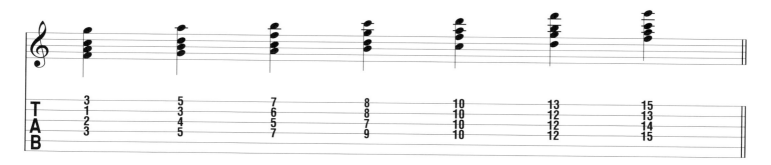

These are slash chord arpeggios from the F and G triad pair.

Track 41

The E and F Triad Pair

Triad pairs can be drawn from other scales. Here the triad pair of E and F, from the A harmonic minor scale, is used. This example shows how the E triad is played over the notes of an F triad.

We can play the following arpeggios based on these slash chords. Use these arpeggios over E7alt.

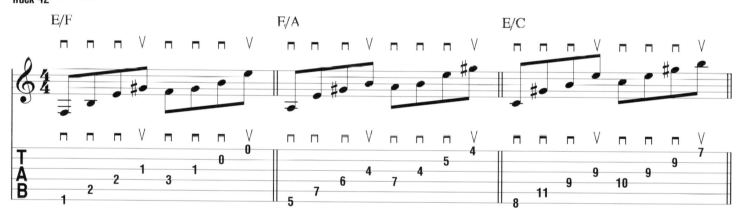

Track 42

For a different sound we can use the foreign tone on top of the voicing. Here the F triad is used with different "bass notes" from the E triad.

We can play the following arpeggios based on F/E, F/G#, and F/B slash chords. Use these
Track 43 arpeggios over E7alt.

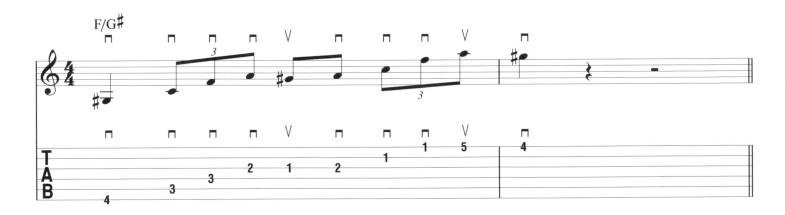

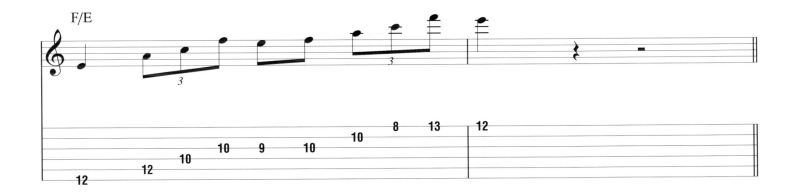

The F and B Triad Pair

The triad pair of F and B is found in the C diminished scale. These lines and chords can be used over C, Eb, Gb, and A diminished chords or over D, F, Ab, and B dominant seventh chords. The F and B triad pair has the chord tones of R 3 5 #11 b7 b9 of F7 (and B7) and #9 5 b7 13 b9 3 of D7 (and Ab7).

Here are F and B triads over a rising bass line, which gives us a variety of slash chords.

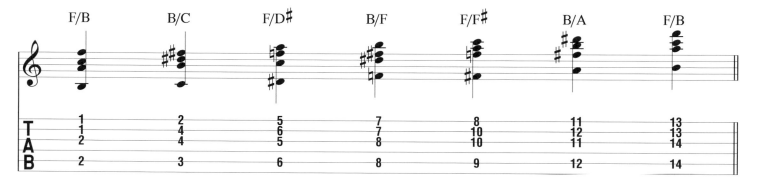

Here are the F and B triads over a rising bass line again, but a tighter harmony results from the triads being closer to the bass line.

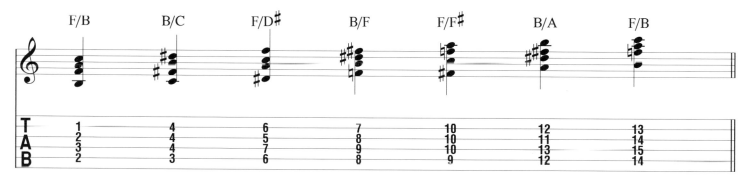

This time the "bass line" is placed on top of the triads.

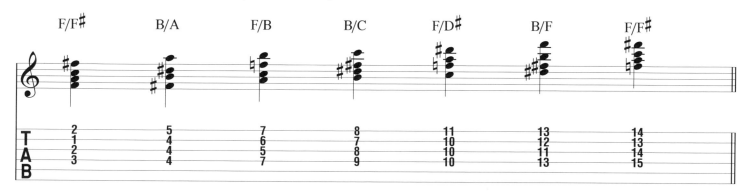

Here are some lines based on the F and B triad pair.

Track 44

We can play the following arpeggios based on B/A, F/B, and B/C slash chords. Use these

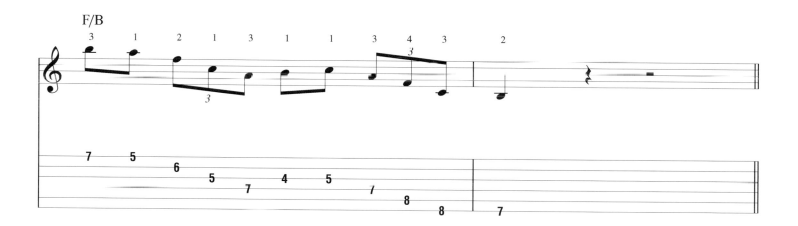

 Track 45 arpeggios over D7, F7, A♭7, and B7.

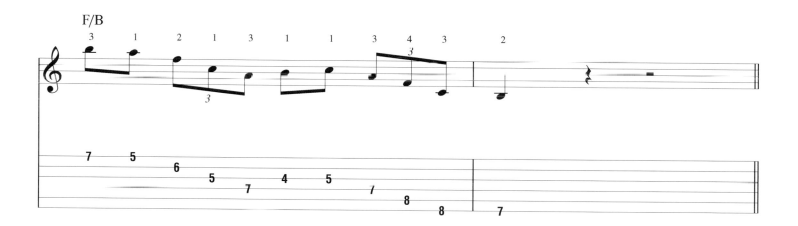

The following arpeggios, based on F/D#, B/F, and F/F# chords, have fingerings that are identical to the previous example due to the triad pair's symmetrical qualities.

Track 46

The F and G aug Triad Pair

A major chord and an augmented chord a whole step higher is the triad pair of choice from the melodic minor mode. Here we'll use F and G augmented, the chords built on the 4th and 5th degrees of the C melodic minor scale. This triad pair works over Cmi6/9, Cmi(ma7), F13(#11), Ami7(b5), and B7alt.

These lines are based on the F and Gaug triad pair, from the C melodic minor scale. The third and fourth lines use a different position and fingering.

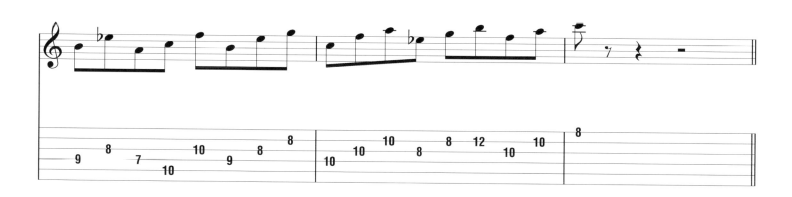

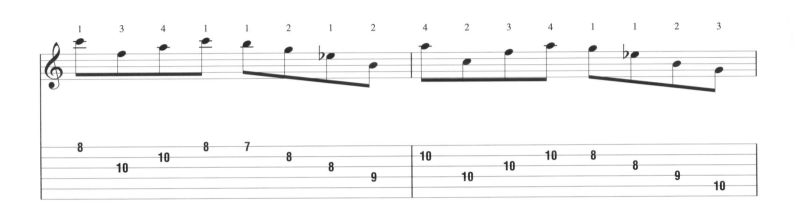

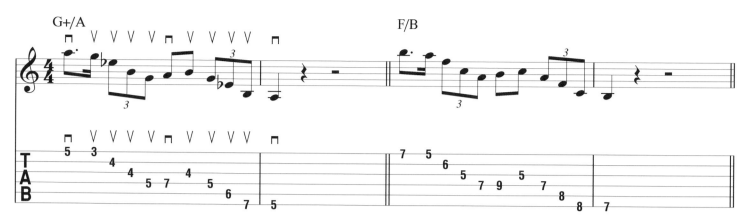

These are some slash chord possibilities using the F and Gaug triad pair over notes from the C melodic minor scale.

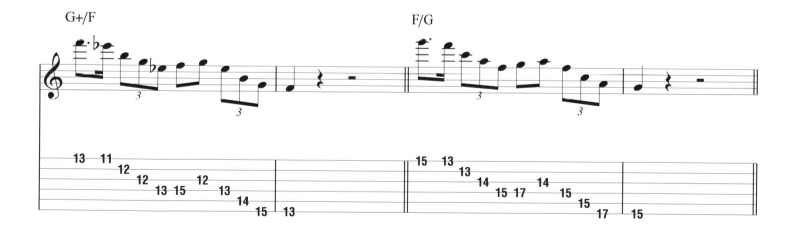

MUSICIANS INSTITUTE PRESS is the official series of Southern California's renowned music school, Musicians Institute. MI instructors, some of the finest musicians in the world, share their vast knowledge and experience with you – no matter what your current level. For guitar, bass, drums, vocals, and keyboards, MI Press offers the finest music curriculum for higher learning through a variety of series:

ESSENTIAL CONCEPTS
Designed from MI core curriculum programs.

MASTER CLASS
Designed from MI elective courses.

PRIVATE LESSONS
Tackle a variety of topics "one-on one" with MI faculty instructors.

GUITAR

Acoustic Artistry
by Evan Hirschelman • Private Lessons
00695922 Book/Online Audio $19.99

Advanced Scale Concepts & Licks for Guitar
by Jean Marc Belkadi • Private Lessons
00695298 Book/CD Pack $19.99

All-in-One Guitar Soloing Course
by Daniel Gilbert & Beth Marlis
00217709 Book/Online Media $29.99

Blues/Rock Soloing for Guitar
by Robert Calva • Private Lessons
00695680 Book/CD Pack $19.99

Blues Guitar Soloing
by Keith Wyatt • Master Class
00695132 Book/Online Audio $29.99

Blues Rhythm Guitar
by Keith Wyatt • Master Class
00695131 Book/Online Audio $19.99

Dean Brown
00696002 DVD $29.95

Chord Progressions for Guitar
by Tom Kolb • Private Lessons
00695664 Book/Online Audio $19.99

Chord Tone Soloing
by Barrett Tagliarino • Private Lessons
00695855 Book/Online Audio $24.99

Chord-Melody Guitar
by Bruce Buckingham • Private Lessons
00695646 Book/Online Audio $19.99

Classical & Fingerstyle Guitar Techniques
by David Oakes • Master Class
00695171 Book/Online Audio $19.99

Classical Themes for Electric Guitar
by Jean Marc Belkadi • Private Lessons
00695806 Book/CD Pack $15.99

Country Guitar
by Al Bonhomme • Master Class
00695661 Book/Online Audio $19.99

Diminished Scale for Guitar
by Jean Marc Belkadi • Private Lessons
00695227 Book/CD Pack $14.99

Essential Rhythm Guitar
by Steve Trovato • Private Lessons
00695181 Book/CD Pack $16.99

Exotic Scales & Licks for Electric Guitar
by Jean Marc Belkadi • Private Lessons
00695860 Book/CD Pack $16.95

Funk Guitar
by Ross Bolton • Private Lessons
00695419 Book/CD Pack $15.99

Guitar Basics
by Bruce Buckingham • Private Lessons
00695134 Book/Online Audio $17.99

Guitar Fretboard Workbook
by Barrett Tagliarino • Essential Concepts
00695712 . . . . $19.99

Guitar Hanon
by Peter Deneff • Private Lessons
00695321 . . . . $14.99

Guitar Lick•tionary
by Dave Hill • Private Lessons
00695482 Book/CD Pack $21.99

Guitar Soloing
by Dan Gilbert & Beth Marlis • Essential Concepts
00695190 Book/CD Pack $22.99

Harmonics
by Jamie Findlay • Private Lessons
00695169 Book/CD Pack $13.99

Harmony & Theory
by Keith Wyatt & Carl Schroeder • Essential Concepts
00695169 . . . . $22.99

Introduction to Jazz Guitar Soloing
by Joe Elliott • Master Class
00695161 Book/Online Audio $19.95

Jazz Guitar Chord System
by Scott Henderson • Private Lessons
00695291 . . . . $12.99

Jazz Guitar Improvisation
by Sid Jacobs • Master Class
00217711 Book/Online Media $19.99

Jazz, Rock & Funk Guitar
by Dean Brown • Private Lessons
00217690 Book/Online Media $19.99

Jazz-Rock Triad Improvising
by Jean Marc Belkadi • Private Lessons
00695361 Book/CD Pack $15.99

Latin Guitar
by Bruce Buckingham • Master Class
00695379 Book/Online Audio $17.99

Lead Sheet Bible
by Robin Randall & Janice Peterson • Private Lessons
00695130 Book/CD Pack $22.99

Liquid Legato
by Allen Hinds • Private Lessons
00696656 Book/Online Audio $16.99

Modern Jazz Concepts for Guitar
by Sid Jacobs • Master Class
00695711 Book/CD Pack $16.95

Modern Rock Rhythm Guitar
by Danny Gill • Private Lessons
00695682 Book/Online Audio $19.99

Modes for Guitar
by Tom Kolb • Private Lessons
00695555 Book/Online Audio $18.99

Music Reading for Guitar
by David Oakes • Essential Concepts
00695192 . . . . $19.99

The Musician's Guide to Recording Acoustic Guitar
by Dallan Beck • Master Class
00695505 Book/CD Pack $13.99

Outside Guitar Licks
by Jean Marc Belkadi • Private Lessons
00695697 Book/CD Pack $16.99

Power Plucking
by Dale Turner • Private Lesson
00695962 Book/CD Pack $19.95

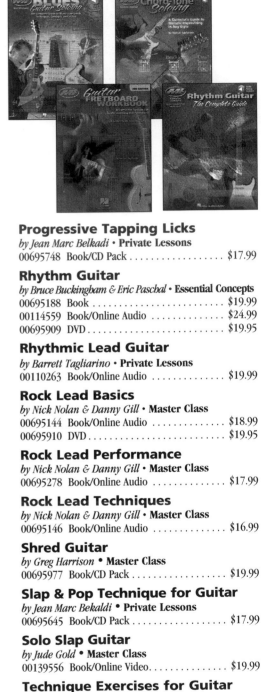

Progressive Tapping Licks
by Jean Marc Belkadi • Private Lessons
00695748 Book/CD Pack $17.99

Rhythm Guitar
by Bruce Buckingham & Eric Paschal • Essential Concepts
00695188 Book $19.99
00114559 Book/Online Audio $24.99
00695909 DVD $19.95

Rhythmic Lead Guitar
by Barrett Tagliarino • Private Lessons
00110263 Book/Online Audio $19.99

Rock Lead Basics
by Nick Nolan & Danny Gill • Master Class
00695144 Book/Online Audio $18.99
00695910 DVD $19.95

Rock Lead Performance
by Nick Nolan & Danny Gill • Master Class
00695278 Book/Online Audio $17.99

Rock Lead Techniques
by Nick Nolan & Danny Gill • Master Class
00695146 Book/Online Audio $16.99

Shred Guitar
by Greg Harrison • Master Class
00695977 Book/CD Pack $19.99

Slap & Pop Technique for Guitar
by Jean Marc Bekaldi • Private Lessons
00695645 Book/CD Pack $17.99

Solo Slap Guitar
by Jude Gold • Master Class
00139556 Book/Online Video $19.99

Technique Exercises for Guitar
by Jean Marc Belkadi • Private Lessons
00695913 Book/CD Pack $15.99

Texas Blues Guitar
by Robert Calva • Private Lessons
00695340 Book/Online Audio $17.99

Ultimate Guitar Technique
by Bill LaFleur • Private Lessons
00695863 Book/Online Audio $22.99

Prices, contents, and availability subject to change without notice.

7777 W. BLUEMOUND RD. P.O. BOX 13819 MILWAUKEE, WI 53213

www.halleonard.com

Musicians Institute Press is the official series of instructional publications from Southern California's renowned music school, Musicians Institute. These books, book/audio packages, and videos have been created by MI instructors who are among the world's best and most experienced professional musicians.

KEYBOARD

00695708	Blues Hanon by Peter Deneff	$17.99
00695556	Dictionary of Keyboard Grooves by Gail Johnson – Book/CD	$16.95
00202430	Easy Jazz Hanon by Peter Deneff – Book/Audio	$12.99
00695336	Funk Keyboards – The Complete Method by Gail Johnson – Book/Audio	$16.99
00695936	Hip-Hop Keyboard by Henry Soleh Brewer Book/CD	$17.95
00695791	Jazz Chord Hanon by Peter Deneff	$17.99
00695554	Jazz Hanon by Peter Deneff	$16.99
00695773	Jazz Piano by Christian Klikovits – Book/CD	$19.99
00695209	Keyboard Voicings by Kevin King	$12.95
00266448	Modal Hanon by Peter Deneff	$14.99
00145419	Pop Keyboard Concepts by Christian Klikovits – Book/Audio	$19.99
00695509	Pop Rock Keyboards by Henry Sol-Eh Brewer & David Garfield – Book/CD	$19.95
00695784	Rock Hanon by Peter Deneff	$19.99
00695226	Salsa Hanon by Peter Deneff	$17.99
00695939	Samba Hanon by Peter Deneff	$16.99
00695882	Stride Hanon by Peter Deneff	$17.99

VOICE

00695883	Advanced Vocal Technique by Dena Murray and Tita Hutchison – Book/Audio	$19.99
00695262	Harmony Vocals by Mike Campbell & Tracee Lewis – Book/Audio	$19.99
00695626	The Musician's Guide to Recording Vocals by Dallan Beck – Book/CD	$15.99
00695629	Rock Vocals by Coreen Sheehan – Book/CD	$17.99
00695195	Sightsinging by Mike Campbell	$19.99
00695427	Vocal Technique by Dena Murray – Book/Audio	$24.99

GUITAR

00695922	Acoustic Artistry by Evan Hirschelman – Book/Audio	$19.99
00695298	Advanced Scale Concepts and Licks for Guitar by Jean Marc Belkadi – Book/CD	$17.99
00217709	All-in-One Guitar Soloing Course by Daniel Gilbert & Beth Marlis	$29.99
00695132	Blues Guitar Soloing by Keith Wyatt – Book/Online Media	$24.99
00695680	Blues/Rock Soloing for Guitar by Robert Calva – Book/Audio	$19.99
00695131	Blues Rhythm Guitar by Keith Wyatt – Book/Audio	$19.99
00696002	Modern Techniques for the Electric Guitarist by Dean Brown – DVD	$29.95
00695664	Chord Progressions for Guitar by Tom Kolb – Book/CD	$17.99
00695855	Chord Tone Soloing by Barrett Tagliarino – Book/Audio	$24.99
00695646	Chord-Melody Guitar by Bruce Buckingham – Book/CD	$19.99
00695171	Classical & Fingerstyle Guitar Techniques by David Oakes – Book/Audio	$17.99
00695806	Classical Themes for Electric Guitar by Jean Marc Belkadi – Book/CD	$15.99
00695661	Country Guitar by Al Bonhomme – Book/Audio	$19.99

00695227	The Diminished Scale for Guitar by Jean Marc Belkadi – Book/CD	$14.99
00695181	Essential Rhythm Guitar by Steve Trovato – Book/CD	$15.99
00695873	Ethnic Rhythms for Electric Guitar by Jean Marc Belkadi – Book/CD	$17.99
00695860	Exotic Scales & Licks for Electric Guitar by Jean Marc Belkadi – Book/CD	$16.95
00695419	Funk Guitar by Ross Bolton – Book/Audio	$15.99
00695134	Guitar Basics by Bruce Buckingham – Book/Audio	$17.99
00695712	Guitar Fretboard Workbook by Barrett Tagliarino	$19.99
00695321	Guitar Hanon by Peter Deneff	$14.99
00695482	The Guitar Lick•tionary by Dave Hill – Book/CD	$19.99
00695190	Guitar Soloing by Daniel Gilbert and Beth Marlis – Book/Audio	$22.99
00695169	Harmonics by Jamie Findlay – Book/CD	$13.99
00695406	Introduction to Jazz Guitar Soloing by Joe Elliott – Book/Audio	$19.95
00695291	Jazz Guitar Chord System by Scott Henderson	$12.99
00217711	Jazz Guitar Improvisation by Sid Jacobs – Book/Online Media	$19.99
00217690	Jazz, Rock & Funk Guitar by Dean Brown – Book/Online Media	$19.99
00695361	Jazz-Rock Triad Improvising for Guitar by Jean Marc Belkadi – Book/CD	$15.99
00695379	Latin Guitar by Bruce Buckingham – Book/Audio	$17.99
00696656	Liquid Legato by Allen Hinds – Book/CD	$14.99
00695143	A Modern Approach to Jazz, Rock & Fusion Guitar by Jean Marc Belkadi – Book/CD	$15.99
00695711	Modern Jazz Concepts for Guitar by Sid Jacobs – Book/CD	$16.95
00695682	Modern Rock Rhythm Guitar by Danny Gill – Book/CD	$16.95
00695555	Modes for Guitar by Tom Kolb – Book/Audio	$18.99
00695192	Music Reading for Guitar by David Oakes	$19.99
00695697	Outside Guitar Licks by Jean Marc Belkadi – Book/CD	$16.99
00695962	Power Plucking by Dale Turner – Book/CD	$19.95
00695748	Progressive Tapping Licks by Jean Marc Belkadi – Book/CD	$16.99
00114559	Rhythm Guitar by Bruce Buckingham & Eric Paschal – Book/Audio	$24.99
00695188	Rhythm Guitar by Bruce Duckingham & Eric Paschal – Book	$19.99
00695909	Rhythm Guitar featuring Bruce Buckingham – DVD	$19.95
00110263	Rhythmic Lead Guitar by Barrett Tagliarino – Book/Audio	$19.99
00695144	Rock Lead Basics by Nick Nolan and Danny Gill – Book/Audio	$18.99
00695278	Rock Lead Performance by Nick Nolan and Danny Gill – Book/Audio	$17.99
00695146	Rock Lead Techniques by Nick Nolan and Danny Gill – Book/Audio	$16.99
00695977	Shred Guitar by Greg Harrison – Book/Audio	$19.99
00139556	Solo Slap Guitar by Jude Gold – Book/Video	$19.99
00695645	Slap & Pop Technique for Guitar by Jean Marc Belkadi – Book/CD	$16.99
00695913	Technique Exercises for Guitar by Jean Marc Belkadi – Book/CD	$15.99
00695340	Texas Blues Guitar by Robert Calva – Book/Audio	$17.99
00695863	Ultimate Guitar Technique by Bill LaFleur – Book/Audio	$22.99

BASS

DRUMS

ALL INSTRUMENTS/OTHER

RECORDING

HAL•LEONARD®

www.halleonard.com

Prices, contents and availability subject to change without notice.